THIS BOOK BELONGS TO:

_____

THE WONDERFUL WORLD OF CAPYBARAS

MIMI JONES

Dedicated to all who love capybaras!

ISBN 978-1-958985-72-4

www.joeysavestheday.com

A Mimi Book

Meet the capybara: the world's biggest rodent!

Capybaras are closely related to guinea pigs but can weigh up to 150 pounds, which is the size of a large dog!

6

Capybaras come from South America and their name means "Grass Eater."

They can be found in grassy wetlands and forests near rivers, lakes, and swamps.

Capybaras have rough, bristly fur that helps them dry quickly after being in water.

Like most rodents, capybaras have four large front teeth that never stop growing!

NEVER Stop growing

10

Since their teeth don't stop growing they have to chew things often to keep them short.

Capybaras are most active during dawn and dusk.

Capybaras are great at staying cool when the weather gets hot. They love to splash around and relax in water, or even wallow in mud to beat the heat.

Their webbed feet make them excellent swimmers, perfect for cooling off in rivers and ponds!

Capybaras can hold their breath for up to five minutes underwater and this clever trick helps them hide from predators by staying completely still beneath the water's surface.

Capybaras are herbivores which means they only eat plants.

Their favorite foods are grasses, fruit, and water plants.

Capybaras are very social animals and live in groups of 10-20 capybaras, sometimes even more!

10 - 20

These groups are called herds.

Capybaras are very clean animals and often groom each other.

CHiRP

Whistle

PURR

Capybaras chirp, whistle, and purr to talk to each other.

Baby capybaras are called pups!

Capybaras can have litters of 2-8 pups.

2 TO 8

In a capybara herd, all the females work together to help take care of the babies.

Pups are able to walk and swim right after they're born.

They start eating grass within a week of being born.

Capybaras can live up to 8-10 years in the wild and even longer in captivity.

People all over the world love capybaras for being calm, friendly, and super cute!

Stay Calm

Capybaras get along well with humans
and many other animals.

Many animals like to sit or perch on capybaras. Birds, monkeys, and even cats have been seen riding on them!

Capybaras are not endangered, but they need clean habitats to thrive.

✖ DON'T LITTER ✖

Protect Habitats

Count the capybaras!

Thank you for exploring the chill and wonderful world of capybaras with us! We hope you had as much fun as a capybara relaxing in the water. If you enjoyed this book, tell your friends and maybe leave a little review.

Check out these other interesting books in the Wonderful World of series!

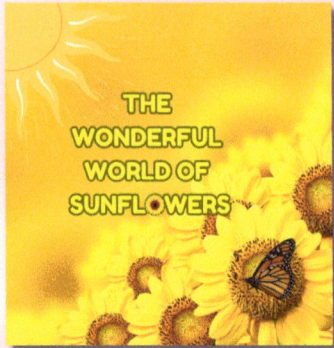

THE WONDERFUL WORLD OF SUNFLOWERS

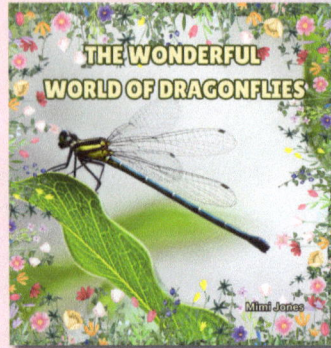

THE WONDERFUL WORLD OF DRAGONFLIES
Mimi Jones

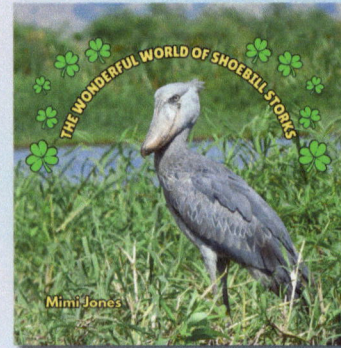

THE WONDERFUL WORLD OF SHOEBILL STORKS
Mimi Jones

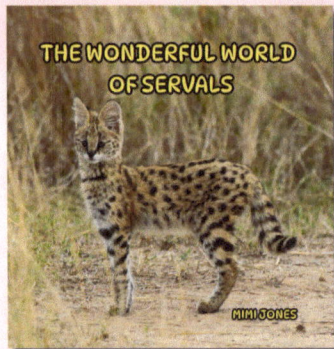

THE WONDERFUL WORLD OF SERVALS
MIMI JONES

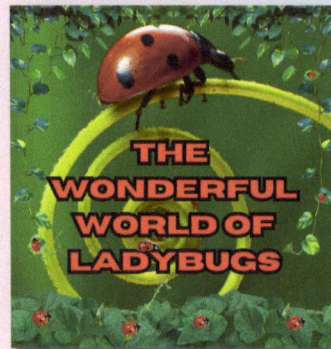

THE WONDERFUL WORLD OF LADYBUGS

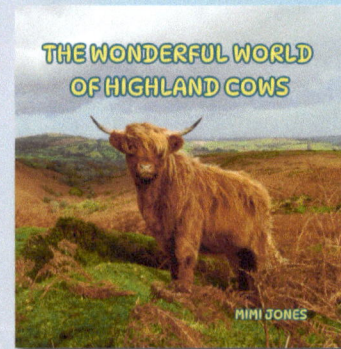

THE WONDERFUL WORLD OF HIGHLAND COWS
MIMI JONES

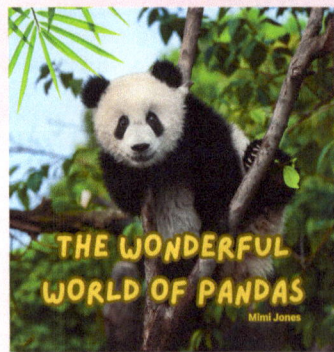

THE WONDERFUL WORLD OF PANDAS
Mimi Jones

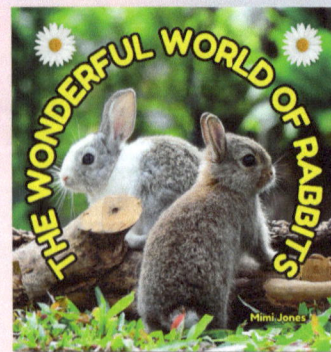

THE WONDERFUL WORLD OF RABBITS
Mimi Jones

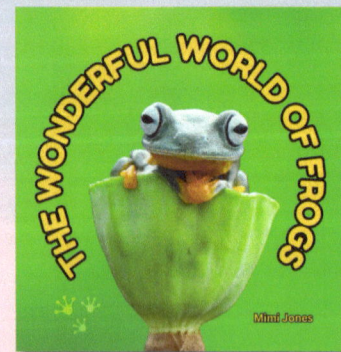

THE WONDERFUL WORLD OF FROGS
Mimi Jones

www.mimibooks.com

www.ingramcontent.com/pod-product-compliance
Lightning Source LLC
Chambersburg PA
CBHW041551040426

42447CB00002B/135